The Alps

By Lynn Peppas

🌳 Crabtree Publishing Company

www.crabtreebooks.com

Crabtree Publishing Company

www.crabtreebooks.com

Author: Lynn Peppas
Editor: Adrianna Morganelli
Proofreader: Crystal Sikkens
Indexer: Wendy Scavuzzo
Designer: Katherine Berti
Photo researcher: Crystal Sikkens
Project coordinator: Kathy Middleton
**Production coordinator &
  prepress technician**: Katherine Berti

Front cover: The Dolomites mountain range in
the Eastern Alps was declared a natural
heritage site in 2009.

Title page: The Swiss Alps is home to the
famous Matterhorn mountain.

Picture credits:
© Hemis/Alamy: p. 40
Katherine Berti: p. 20–21 (mountain)
Dreamstime: p. 9, 39
Margaret Amy Salter: p. 21 (snowflakes)
Samara Parent: p. 5
Shutterstock: cover, p. 1, 4, 5, 7 (top), 8, 10, 14, 15, 16, 17, 18,
    19, 22, 23, 24, 25 (top), 26, 27, 28 (top), 29, 30, 31, 34, 38,
    40 (bottom), 41, 42, 43, 44, 45
Wikimedia Commons: Eric Bajart: p. 32 (bottom); Benh
    Lieu Song: p. 32 (top); Franco Christophe: p. 25 (bottom);
    Daniel D: p. 33; Jacques-Louis David—Kunsthistorisches
    Museum: p. 37 (Napoleon); Jo in Riederalp: p. 12;
    Lencer—United States National Imagery and Mapping
    Agency data—Generic Mapping Tools (GMT) with
    SRTM3 V2 Relief-Files: p. 6; Lenny222: p. 14 (top); Philip
    James de Loutherbourg the Younger—Tate Britain:
    p. 36–37 (mountain); Jeff Pang: p. 7 (bottom); Dr. Michel
    Royon: p. 28 (bottom); A. Stafiniak: p. 13; United States
    Geological Survel: p. 11 (bottom)

Library and Archives Canada Cataloguing in Publication

Peppas, Lynn
  The Alps / Lynn Peppas.

(Mountains around the world)
Includes index.
Issued also in electronic formats.
ISBN 978-0-7787-7559-1 (bound).--ISBN 978-0-7787-7566-9 (pbk.)

  1. Alps--Juvenile literature. I. Title. II. Series: Mountains around
the world (St. Catharines, Ont.)

DQ823.5.P47 2011   j914.94'7   C2011-905228-8

Library of Congress Cataloging-in-Publication Data

Peppas, Lynn.
  The Alps / Lynn Peppas.
    p. cm. -- (Mountains around the world)
  Includes index.
  ISBN 978-0-7787-7559-1 (reinforced library binding : alk. paper) -- ISBN 978-
0-7787-7566-9 (pbk. : alk. paper) -- ISBN 978-1-4271-8840-3 (electronic PDF) --
ISBN 978-1-4271-9743-6 (electronic HTML)
  1. Natural history--Alps--Juvenile literature. 2. Alps--History--Juvenile
literature. 3. Alps--Environmental conditions--Juvenile literature. 4.
Mountain life--Alps--Juvenile literature. I. Title. II. Series.

  QH175.P43 2012
  508.494'7--dc23
                                                            2011029828

Crabtree Publishing Company

www.crabtreebooks.com   1-800-387-7650

Printed in Canada/092011/MA20110714

Published in Canada
Crabtree Publishing
616 Welland Ave.
St. Catharines, Ontario
L2M 5V6

Published in the United States
Crabtree Publishing
PMB 59051
350 Fifth Avenue, 59th Floor
New York, New York 10118

Published in the United Kingdom
Crabtree Publishing
Maritime House
Basin Road North, Hove
BN41 1WR

Published in Australia
Crabtree Publishing
3 Charles Street
Coburg North
VIC 3058

CONTENTS

Words that are defined in the glossary are in **bold** type
the first time they appear in the text.

CHAPTER 1

The Alps: Europe's Most Popular Peaks

The Alps are not only the largest mountain range in Europe; they are also the most popular. The Alps hold the honor of being the most famous mountain chain on Earth, even though there are taller, wider, and larger mountain ranges throughout the world. More people live in and around the Alps than any other mountain range on Earth. They are also the most visited by tourists.

Tourists visit the Alps in both the winter and summer seasons.

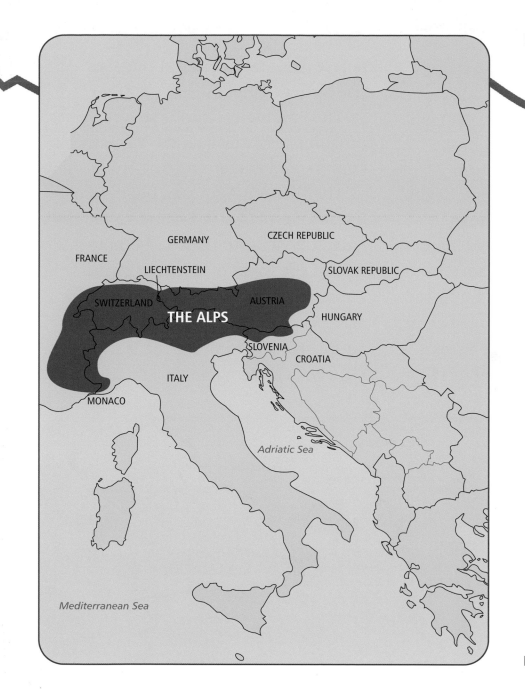

The map shows THE ALPS spanning across FRANCE, MONACO, SWITZERLAND, LIECHTENSTEIN, GERMANY, ITALY, AUSTRIA, SLOVENIA, and near CZECH REPUBLIC, SLOVAK REPUBLIC, HUNGARY, CROATIA, the Adriatic Sea, and Mediterranean Sea.

What is a Mountain?

A mountain is a gigantic natural landform that rises above Earth's surface. A mountain often has steep sides rising to a summit, which is the highest point or peak. Mountains are usually found in long ranges or groups of ranges called chains. They are formed in different ways, but most of the mountains on Earth have formed over millions of years. You may not be able to notice or feel it, but mountains are forming even as you read this book!

World-Famous Name

Why are the Alps so famous? Part of the Alps' fame comes from having been the first mountain range to ever be studied by **geologists**. Many geologic mountain and glacier terms originated from these early studies of the Alps.

Even the word, alps, has been borrowed by other mountain ranges, such as the Australian Alps.

Even though this range uses the name, "Alps," they are an entirely different mountain range, found in an entirely different country of Australia. The "Alps" name comes from the **Latin** word "*alpes*" that means "high mountains." For this reason, the word "alpine" is used to describe the highest altitude area of mountains or things related to high, mountainous regions.

The Heart of Europe

The mountain ranges of the Alps stretch for over 660 miles (1,000 km) throughout seven countries in the continent of Europe. They form a curve from east to west, that begins in Slovenia, and travels through Austria, Italy, Germany, Liechtenstein, Switzerland, and ends in France.

They vary in width from 80 to 150 miles (130 to 240 km). They cover an area of about 85,000 square miles (220,000 square km). Several of the tallest mountain peaks in the Alps rise to over 10,000 feet (3,000 m).

The mountain chain is divided into three ranges known as the Western, Central, and Eastern Alps.

The Western Alps area begins from the southern area in France, called the French Riviera, to the southernmost side of the Great St. Bernard Pass. These mountain ranges consist of high, narrow mountains. From south to north, the divisions are the Maritime, Ligurian, Cottian, and Graian alps.

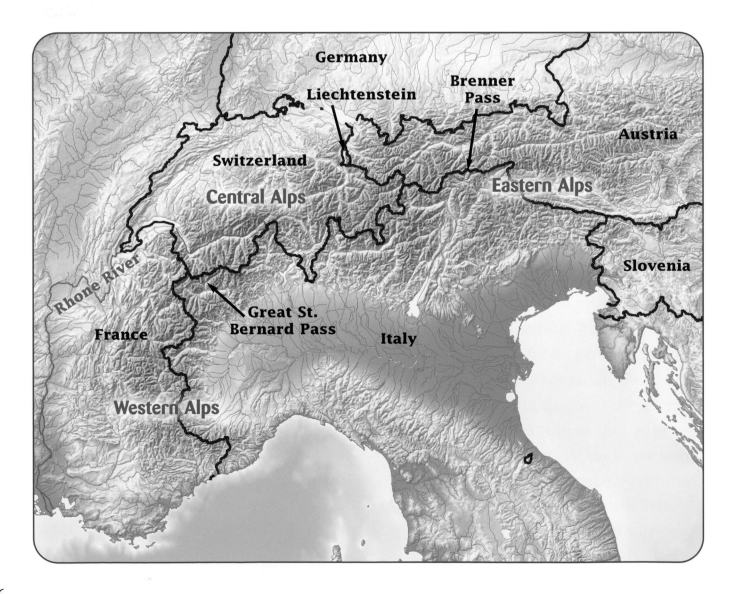

The Savoy mountains are part of the Western Alps in southeast France.

The Central Alps area begins from the Great St. Bernard Pass and travels eastward toward the Brenner Pass, on the border of Italy and Austria. These mountain ranges include some of the highest mountain peaks in the Alps. From south of the Rhone River, the divisions are the Pennine, Lepontine, Phaetian, and Otztal alps. North of the Rhone River, the divisions are the Bernina, Glarus, Allgau, and Bavarian alps.

The Matterhorn is a famous mountain in the Central Alps.

Finally, the Eastern Alps are found in Italy, Austria, and Germany. The area extends eastward from the Brenner Pass in Austria, to Slovenia. These mountain regions are not as high as the others, but are the broadest and some span 150 miles (240 km) across. To the south, the divisions are the Dolomites and the Carnic and Julian Alps, and the Hohe Tauern and Niedere Tauern are in the northern area of Austria.

The Dolomites, in Italy, are a well-known mountain range of the Eastern Alps.

NOTABLE QUOTE

"It is not only the lover of natural beauty who finds pleasure and satisfaction in the Alps…the poet and the painter have been stimulated by them to a higher sense of the glories of nature, and for science the Alps are truly classic ground. It was in the Alps that modern geology made its first essays, and it was by the study of the problems which they offered that it grew to its prominent position among the sciences."

—From *The Alps* by Friedrich Umlauft, translated by Louisa Brough, published in 1889.

This tourist spot gives visitors a look at some of the Swiss Alps' cliffs. Cliffs like these are often created by falling rocks and erosion.

FAST FACT
Scientists estimate that in one year the Alps gain about the width of a penny, or one millimeter, in height. The Alps also erode due to melting ice and falling rock. The two seem to cancel each other out and they remain about the same height.

CHAPTER 2

Peaks and Passes of the Alps

The Alps are the youngest mountain range in Europe. Geologists believe they were formed about 30 to 40 million years ago. That may seem like a very long time ago, but some mountain ranges on Earth were formed over 500 million years ago!

The folding process that formed the Alps didn't happen suddenly, but occurred over millions of years.

Fold Mountains

Different mountain ranges are formed by different processes. The Alps are "fold" or folded mountains. They were formed by a buckling, or upward folding, of Earth's **crust**.

Earth's surface is covered with floating **tectonic plates**. These plates cover Earth like huge puzzle pieces. The Alps were formed when two of Earth's tectonic plates, the Eurasian plate and the African plate, crashed and began pushing against each other.

Millions of years ago, the Eurasian plate and the African plate were separated by a body of water called the Tethys Sea. When these huge plates moved toward one another, they pushed and folded Earth's crust upward to form the Alps mountain range. Part of the pushed-up crust included the seafloor of the Tethys Sea. Geologists discovered this when **fossils** of sea animals such as ammonites were found on the Alps' mountain peaks.

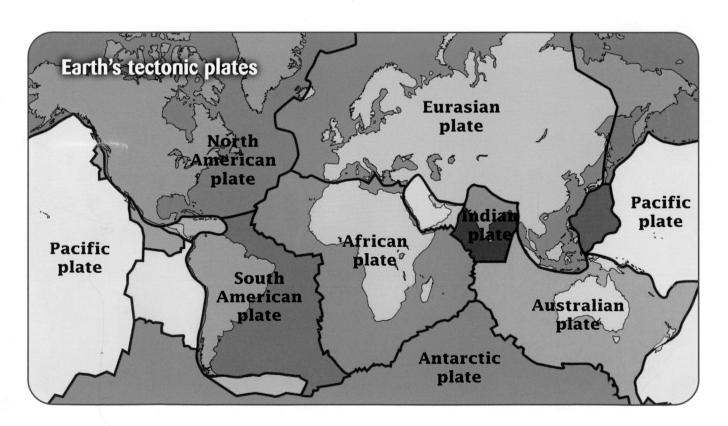

Earth's tectonic plates

Glaciers of The Alps

During the last ice age, which ended just over 10,000 years ago, much of Earth was covered with glaciers. Glaciers are frozen rivers made of layers of ice that grow with every snowfall. As the snow falls, it compresses the layer of snow underneath into ice. Glaciers are pulled downhill by gravity. As these heavy glaciers slowly move downhill they pull rocks and soil along with them. Glaciers carve out valleys, hills, and ridges called **moraines**. Glaciers carved out the many lakes that are nestled amongst the Alps such as Lake Como in Italy. In Switzerland, the Hornli ridge on top of the Matterhorn mountain is the most famous example of a mountain peak formed by the incredible cutting power of a glacier.

Glaciers still exist today on the highest mountaintops in the Alps. The Aletsch Glacier is the largest glacier in the Alps. It is on Jungfrau mountain in Switzerland. The Aletsch Glacier is over 14 miles (23 km) long and is over half a mile (one km) deep. This massive glacier feeds the Massa River.

Mountain Passes and Tunnels: Getting Over It

Mountains are natural barriers between countries and people, but they can be crossed over. Since ancient times, people have been traveling over mountain ranges through mountain passes. A mountain pass is a pathway or route between mountain peaks or summits. The pass is the highest point of the pathway.

There are hundreds of passes throughout the Alps mountain range. One of the most famous passes is the Great St. Bernard Pass. It is also the oldest known pass in the Alps. It was used by travelers over 2,500 years ago. It is also one of the highest passes throughout the Alps mountain range.

The pass is located over 8,000 feet (2,500 m) in Switzerland. It connects Italy to Switzerland. The Great St. Bernard Pass is the lowest pathway between the Alps's two highest mountains, Mont Blanc and Monte Rosa.

Sometimes it is easier to travel through a mountain rather than over it. A tunnel is a human-made route that cuts through the base of a mountain. In 2010, the Alps became home to the world's longest land tunnel. The Loetschberg Base Tunnel is 21 miles (34 km) long. It was built for train travel in Switzerland. The Gotthard Road Tunnel is another tunnel found in Switzerland. It is over ten miles (16 km) in length. It is the third longest road tunnel in the world.

People have been traveling on the Great St. Bernard Pass for thousands of years.

High Points of the Alps

A "four-thousander" is the name for a mountain that measures 4,000 meters (13,123 feet) or taller. Not all of the mountains in the Alps measure this height, but many exceed it. Mountains such as Mont Blanc, Monte Rosa, the Finsteraarhorn, the Weisshorn, and over 120 other mountains in the Alps are members of the Alpine "four-thousander" group.

The tallest mountain peak, or summit, in the Alps is Mont Blanc. Three countries, France, Italy, and Switzerland share this mountain. In both Italian and French languages, the name means "white mountain." It is the 11th tallest mountain in the world. It stands over 15,780 feet (4,810 m) tall.

The Matterhorn is a "four-thousander" with a height of 14,692 feet (4,478 m). It was carved by the movement of glaciers thousands of years ago, and is a popular challenge for mountain climbers because of its steep, rocky ridge.

The very first Winter Olympic Games were held on Mont Blanc. It was hosted by a city named Chamonix, in France, in 1924.

NOTABLE QUOTE

"Far, far above, piercing the infinite sky,
Mont Blanc appears—still, snowy, and serene
Its subject mountains their unearthly forms
Pile around it, ice and rock; broad vales between…"

—From the poem, "Mont Blanc," by 17th century poet, Percy Bysshe Shelley

Drainage Basins of the Alps

The Alps not only look beautiful, they are also an important source of freshwater for Europe. The Alps provide about 40 percent of Europe's freshwater. Freshwater comes from melting snow and ice on the mountains. Water from the mountains drain into four main river **drainage basins**. These basins form some of the largest rivers found in Europe. They are the Rhine, Rhone, and Po rivers. These rivers split and feed smaller rivers that provide freshwater throughout Europe. Their final destination is to flow into the Mediterranean, Adriatic, or Black Sea. These rivers are important for drinking water, industries, and hydroelectric power.

(above) The Rhine River collects **watershed** from Alps' mountains in Switzerland. It begins at the Rheinwaldhorn glacier. From Switzerland the Rhine River flows through the European countries of Germany, Italy, Austria, Liechtenstein, and France. It is over 760 miles (1,200 km) long, making it one of the longest rivers in Europe. It drains into the North Sea from the Netherlands.

(left) The Rhone River also collects watershed from the Alps in Switzerland. From Switzerland it flows through the European country of France. It is over 500 miles (800 km) long, and drains into the Mediterranean Sea from France.

(right) The Po River flows through Italy. It begins at Monte Viso, a mountain in the Alps. It is over 400 miles (650 km) long, and drains into the Adriatic Sea from Venice, Italy.

Drainage basins, such as this one in Germany, collect freshwater from the Alps to form some of the largest rivers in Europe.

17

CHAPTER 3
Climate of the Alps

Mountains have their own **climate** because of their great height. A mountain, by definition, is a landform that stands 980 feet (300 m) or taller. In the Alps mountain range, the average height of a mountain is well over 7,000 feet (2,000 m). The climate of the Alps, and other large mountain ranges, is called a highland climate.

The Alps are a large mountain chain that spread for over 660 miles (1,000 km). The climate changes in different areas. The Alps in the southern region have a hot, dry climate in the summer, and mild winters, such as in the Alps of southern France and Italy. The Alps in the northern region have a **temperate** climate with warm summers and cold winters such as in the Alps of Austria.

High mountains, such as Mont Blanc, have snow on them even during the hot summer months.

Temperature Changes

A mountain's climate changes at different heights. The climate gets colder at higher **altitudes**, or greater heights. The temperature is about one degree cooler as the altitude increases by 300 feet (100 m). Some of the highest mountain peaks of the Alps mountains are snow- and ice-covered all year round.

Air cools as it rises. This is because a layer of gases surrounds Earth called the atmosphere. These gases include air needed for life on Earth. Earth's atmosphere is held in place by gravity. As altitude increases, gravity has less of a pull on the atmosphere, and air molecules spread farther apart. Air becomes thinner. Thinner air holds less heat and the temperature decreases.

Thinner air also holds less **oxygen**. Mountain climbers often carry oxygen with them to help them breathe when they are climbing at high altitudes.

FAST FACT
About two percent of the Alps are covered year-round by ice.

NOTABLE QUOTE

"...My own delights; the lordly Alps themselves, Those rosy peaks, from which the Morning looks Abroad on many nations..."

—From "The Prelude" or "Growth of a Poet" by William Wordsworth

19

Mountain Winds

The height of the Alps mountain range creates a wind barrier. A mountain changes the flow of air that continuously travels across Earth called **prevailing winds**. The side of a mountain that has the wind blowing against it is called the windward side. The side of a mountain with the wind blowing away from it is called the leeward side.

Foehn Wind

Winds that blow away from the leeward side of the Alps mountains are called Foehn winds. Foehn winds are dry because the moisture has been squeezed out of the air on the windward side of the mountain. As the wind travels down the mountain it becomes warmer and soaks up the moisture from the ground. This creates very dry areas and is called a rain shadow. A Foehn wind is a rain shadow wind.

In the Zone

There are five different climate zones in the Alps. They are determined by altitude. These climate changes vary so much that they affect the type of plants and wildlife that live in these zones. The lowland zone is at the bottom, or base, of a mountain. Lowlands are found below 3,200 feet (975 m). This area has the lowest altitude and therefore has the warmest climate. The arable zone is located between 3,200 feet (975 m) and 5,000 feet (1,524 m). The subalpine zone is found from 5,000 feet (1,524 m) to 6,500 feet (1,981 m). The alpine zone is located between 6,500 feet (1,981 m) and 9,800 feet (2,987 m). During the summer season, the average temperature is around 50 degrees Fahrenheit (10 degrees Celsius) during the daytime. However, during the night temperatures often drop below freezing, 32 degrees Fahrenheit (0 degrees Celsius). The névé zone is the area located above 9,800 feet (2,987 m) and has the coldest climate on a mountain. This area is covered in snow and ice all year round.

Névé zone

Alpine zone

Subalpine zone

Arable zone

Lowlands

Rain and Snow

Mountains also act as a precipitation barrier. As wind blows it carries warm air up the windward side of a mountain. Warm air holds the most moisture, or water. As the warm air travels up a mountain the air becomes cooler and less able to hold water. This water falls in the form of precipitation such as rain or snow. This weather process is called orographic lift. There is much more rainfall and snow found on the windward side of the Alps mountain range.

Snow Line

The snow line is a boundary, above which snow and ice exist all year round. In the Alps, the altitude of the snow line depends on the location of the mountain. Mountains found in the southern region have warmer climates and therefore the snow line is found at a higher altitude around 9,000 feet (2,743 m). Mountains in the more northern regions of the Alps have snow lines at lower altitudes of around 8,200 feet (2,500 m).

CHAPTER 4
Animal and Plant Life

The Alps mountain range is one of the richest biodiversities of plant and animal life in Europe. A biodiversity is an environment with many different **species** of plants and animals. Part of the reason for the wide variety of living things comes from the different climate zones on the Alps that create different habitats.

There are three mountain areas where plant life exists. Forest areas begin at the base of a mountain and continue upward until the tree line. The tree line is a boundary that marks where trees are able to grow. From the tree line up, meadow areas exist. Further up rockier areas feature the hardiest plants and animals. At higher altitudes above the snow line, at around 10,000 feet (3,048 m), precipitation remains year-round in the form of ice or snow. This is a barren area where no plants or animals can survive.

This vineyard is at the foot of the Italian Alps. Italy is famous for producing some of the best wines in the world.

Plant Life of the Alps

Many different species of plants grow in different climate zones of the Alps mountain range. As the altitude increases, the temperature becomes colder and the growing season is shorter. At higher altitudes there is also less soil due to precipitation such as rain that washes away the soil.

Forest Area

The forest area found at the base of the Alps mountains is the most temperate. From the base of the mountain up to about 1,600 feet (488 m) farmers grow vineyards of grapes for wine production. The land at lower altitudes is good for farming because the soil is rich from ancient glacier deposits. The climate is the warmest at the lowest altitudes, too.

Trees of the Alps

In the Alps, the average tree line varies from around 5,900 to 7,200 feet (1,798 to 2,194 m), depending on where the mountain is located. The tree line is sometimes called the timberline. On mountains, trees cannot grow at higher altitudes where the climate is colder and the growing season is shorter. As altitude increases, the number, type, and size of trees decrease. Trees cannot grow above the tree line.

Deciduous trees are broad-leafed plants that lose their leaves seasonally. They grow in forest areas. They can survive in the lowland and arable zones of the Alps because they are at the lowest altitudes and are therefore in the warmest areas. These zones have rich soil deposits that have been pushed down by ancient glaciers.

Forests of these trees grow up to an altitude of about 2,000 feet (609 m).

Conifer trees are hardier and can survive at higher altitudes and colder climates of the Alps. Conifer trees have needles that they keep year round. Needles are an **adaptation** that helps them to survive colder climates because the snow slides off them. Needles also help the tree produce food whenever it is sunny. Conifer trees found on the Alps include spruce, fir, and many species of pine such as Scots pine. Conifer trees can grow up to altitudes around 5,900 feet (1,800 m). Shorter pines such as the mountain pine can survive at even higher altitudes of up to 7,200 feet (2,194 m). They are some of the last trees found growing before the tree line.

Tree line

This village in the Swiss Alps has deciduous trees growing around the homes, while conifer trees grow up to the tree line on the mountain.

Meadow Area

Meadows are found in the altitudes above the tree line where forests no longer grow. The Alps are well known for their picturesque meadows and wide variety of colorful wildflowers that grow in these areas. Wildflowers such as edelweiss and alpen rose thrive in these higher altitudes. These wildflowers had to adapt to the rockier conditions of the Alps with strong, shallow root systems that need little soil to grow in. Many alpine plants also grow close to the ground so they are not damaged by strong winds. They have bright flowering blossoms to attract insects that pollinate. Some plants such as lobelia have hair on their leaves to keep them warm.

Edelweiss is a popular plant that grows in the Alps. It is a small, white, star-shaped flowering plant. It has adapted to grow well in rocky soils at high altitudes. It grows best in altitudes from 5,000 to 10,000 feet (1,676 to 3,048 m).

Endemic Plants

There are about 400 species of plants that are endemic to the Alps. Endemic means that a plant or animal naturally grow in one particular location only. The Saxifraga florulenta is an example of an endemic species of plant that grows only in the Alps. This plant is often found growing on rocks at altitudes from 5,500 to 10,000 feet (1,676 m to 3,048 m). It has small, leathery leaves that spiral into a rosette shape. It shoots out a bell-shaped flower stalk with up to 300 tiny, pink flowers on it.

The Saxifraga florulenta can live up to 75 years and flowers only once in its life.

Animal Life in the Alps

Animals live in the forest and meadow areas of the Alps. Animals, like plants, have had to adapt to the harsh mountain conditions of the Alps.

Alpine ibex are a species of wild goat that have sturdy hooves that make them excellent climbers. They have large, curved horns to protect them from predators. They are herbivores that **graze** on grasses that grow in the Alps' meadows. They live in high altitudes of up to 6,500 to 15,000 feet (1,981 to 4,572 m).

The Chamois resemble a cross between a goat and an antelope. They live in Alpine meadows in the Alps from 6,000 feet (1,829 m). They are sure-footed climbers that can easily move about rocky areas.

Both the Alpine ibex (left) and Chamois (right) live in the high, rocky, Alpine meadows of the Alps.

Some animals such as the Alpine marmot **hibernate** during winter months. These small animals, which resemble American groundhogs, hibernate in underground burrows. They huddle together in large groups to keep warm through the winter months.

The Alpine field mouse is an endemic species found only in the Alps. This small rodent lives in rocky, forest, and meadow zones at altitudes of up to 1,600 to 6,900 feet (487 to 2,103 m).

FAST FACT
The Alps are home to over 13,000 plant species and 30,000 animal species. The Alps are known as a European biodiversity "hotspot."

Alpine marmots live in the Alps at altitudes from 2,600 to 10,500 feet (792 to 3,200 m).

Bird Life in the Alps

There are about 200 species of birds that live in the Alps, such as the golden eagle. These large birds can weigh from eight to 15 pounds (four to seven kg). They prey on other animals, such as mice, rabbits, marmots, or small ibex, for food. Although this species once lived throughout Europe, many now live only in **remote** mountain areas such as the Alps. They can live in altitudes of up to 12,000 feet (3,658 m).

Golden eagles tend to mate for life. They build nests called aeries under the tree line usually in rock ledges on the side of the mountain. They often build a few aeries and alternate through them for several years.

aerie

NOTABLE QUOTE

"Where are the eagles and the trumpets?
Buried beneath some snow-deep Alps.
Over buttered scones and crumpets…"

—T. S. Eliot, from the poem, "Cooking Egg" 1920

Animals' Adaptations to Mountain Life

Some animals, such as red deer and Alpine ibex, **migrate** to lower altitudes in the forest areas during winter months to protect themselves from the severe, winter climate of the Alps. When the seasons change and the climate warms, these animals move to higher altitudes in the meadow areas.

At high altitudes the air is much thinner and has less oxygen. Animals that live in high altitudes have adapted to these conditions with larger lungs to help them breathe more air and get more oxygen. These animals also have more red blood cells. Red blood cells carry oxygen inside the body. Animals living in higher altitudes need more red blood cells to help them take more oxygen from the air.

Threat of Extinction

Many animals living in the Alps were faced with extinction during the 1900s. Many species of animals such as the brown bear became endangered when they lost a great deal of their natural habitat due to **urbanization** and tourism. Some species such as the ibex were hunted to near extinction, too. Wildlife conservation agencies such as WWF (World Wildlife Fund) and ALPARC (Alpine Network of Protected Areas) have worked toward the protection of these animals. Today, many species are slowly gaining in population in protected areas of the Alps.

Red deer migrate to escape the harsh winter climate and to find food. They are herbivores that spend most of their day searching and feeding on grasses and plants.

CHAPTER 5

Alpine History, People, and Cultures

The Alps have a long history of attracting people to their majestic mountaintops and beautiful valleys. Almost 14 million people live in the Alps, and they are the most highly populated mountain range in the world. They are also the most visited range and are a popular tourist destination that offers winter and summer sports and recreation.

No other mountain range on Earth has inspired so many classic works of literature and art that still remain popular today. The Alps are also found in seven different European countries. This adds to its rich and interesting diversity of cultures.

In Val Camonica, Italy, pathways and platforms have been constructed to help tourists view the petroglyphs.

Discoveries in the Alps

People have lived and traveled through the Alps mountain range for as long as humans have existed. Scientists have discovered proof that Neanderthals—early relatives of humans—lived in caves in the Alps over 50,000 years ago.

More evidence that people have lived in the Alps comes from petroglyphs crafted by ancient artists over seven thousand years ago. A petroglyph is a carving or drawing that is done on rock. Val Camonica, a valley in the Alps in Italy, is home to one of the largest collection of prehistoric petroglyphs in the world.

Archaeologists have discovered weapons, tools, and clothing that show human life existed high in the Alps over seven thousand years ago. Recent warming trends in the Alps within the past 20 years have melted some of the ice that preserved these artifacts for all those years.

There are over 200,000 engraved figures that can be seen in the rock throughout the valley of Val Camonica, that date as far back as 8,000 years ago.

FAST FACT
In 1991, the remains of a frozen mummy were discovered in the Otztal Alps in Italy. The mummy was a male who had lived over 5,000 years ago. He has been named Otzi the Iceman.

Exploring the Alps

Travelers began exploring the higher regions of the Alps in the late 1400s. An alpine traveler or climber is sometimes called a mountaineer. In the mid-1700s, a Swiss traveler named Horace-Bénédict de Saussure began traveling throughout the Alps to study them. He tried to climb to the top of Mont Blanc in 1785 but failed. He is often called the founder of alpinism, which means to climb and hike in the mountains for sport.

On August 8, 1786, about a year after de Saussure's attempt, Michel-Gabriel Paccard and Jacques Balmat succeeded in climbing Mont Blanc, the Alps' highest mountain.

The Matterhorn was one of the last of the Alps' mountains climbed by mountaineers because it is so dangerous to climb. On July 14, 1865, a party of five English mountaineers reached the summit of the Matterhorn for the first time ever recorded. Unfortunately, four of the climbers died as they were returning down the mountain. Only one mountaineer named Edward Whymper survived.

A commune, or village, in France named Chamonix is situated near the summit of Mont Blanc. Monuments of Michel Gabriel Paccard (above) and Horace-Bénédict de Saussure and Jacques Balmat (opposite) were erected to pay tribute to these mountaineers.

This 20-foot (6 m) high steel sculpture was constructed to pay tribute to English mountaineer, Edward Whymper.

Migrant Cultures

For thousands of years, people living in the Alps have moved from lower to higher ground, depending on the season. This movement, or migration, is called **transhumance**. During warmer, summer months farmers shepherded their animals, such as cows or goats, up the Alps mountains to higher pastures for grazing. During colder months they would return with their livestock to cleared farm areas in the warmer, lowland zones. Today, there are still many farmers making their living in the Alps.

Say "Cheese"

Dairy farmers in the Alps are renowned for their cheese-making abilities. Many areas have created their own types of cheese, such as Switzerland's Gruyere cheese. This popular cheese has been produced in the small town of Gruyeres, Switzerland, for hundreds of years.

Many areas in the Alps celebrate transhumance with festivals such as the Almabtrieb Festival in Wildschonau, Austria. This festival includes a parade of up to 500 cows as they return from their summer pastures in September. Their horns are often decorated with flowers.

The Alps in Wartime

Throughout history, the Alps mountains have given humans a challenge to cross but they are not impossible. In fact, military leaders have marched entire armies over the Alps mountain range.

Over 2,000 years ago an ancient leader named Hannibal and his army crossed the Alps. Hannibal was from the ancient city of Carthage, which today is a city in the country of Tunisia. Hannibal's army crossed the Alps to attack the Romans in 218 B.C. but his exact route is unknown.

In 800 A.D., the Frankish king Charlemagne led his army over the Alps to defeat Italy and become the Roman Emperor.

Another famous general who led the French army across the Alps was Napoleon Bonaparte in 1803. Bonaparte fought against the Austrians who had invaded Italy.

Most recently, armies have fought in the Alps during the First and Second World Wars in the 1900s. During the First World War, from 1914–1918, Italian and Austrian armies fought against one another in the Alps. During the Second World War the German army operated concentration camps, such as the KZ Salzburg-Maxglan concentration camp, at the base of the Alps mountains in Austria.

FAST FACT
Ancient historians, such as Polybius, wrote about Hannibal's army, which included elephants, and their march through the Alps.

NOTABLE QUOTE

"…cottages here and there peeping forth from among the trees, formed a scene of singular beauty. But it was augmented and rendered sublime by the mighty Alps, whose white and shining pyramids and domes towered above all…"

—from *Frankenstein* by Mary Wollstonecraft Shelley

The Alps in the Arts

The Alps are popular in Europe and have inspired great works of art that are still admired and read today. French painter, Jacques-Louis David painted *Napoleon Crossing the Alps* in the early 1800s. In 1803, Philip James de Loutherbourg painted *An Avalanche in the Alps*.

Many classic books are set in the Alps, such as *Heidi's Years of Wandering and Learning*, or *Heidi* for short. Swiss author, Johanna Spyri, wrote *Heidi* in 1880. It is the story of a 5-year-old orphaned girl being raised by her aunt. She is brought to live with her grandfather in the Alps in Switzerland. The story is about Heidi's happy childhood life in the Alps with her grandfather.

Other classic novels set in the Alps include Mary Shelley's novel, *Frankenstein*.

An Avalanche in the Alps by Philip James de Loutherbourg

Shelley wrote this classic novel in the United Kingdom. It was published in 1818. In the novel, Dr. Frankenstein abandons the monster he created by hiding in a valley in the Alps. The monster follows him there.

The Magic Mountain by the German writer Thomas Mann, was published in 1924. This novel tells the story of a young man, Hans Castorp, who visits his ailing cousin in a hospital high up in the Swiss Alps. Hans becomes sick during his visit and ends up recovering at the hospital for seven years.

The Sound of Music is a popular film that tells the story of the von Trappe family who live in Austria. The family escapes the Nazi army at the end of the film by crossing the Alps into Switzerland while singing the song "Climb Every Mountain."

Napoleon Crossing the Alps by Jacques-Louis David

CHAPTER 6
Natural Resources and Tourism

The Alps are Europe's most popular peaks. Millions of people flock to mountain resorts in the Alps for the summer and winter sports. Many people that live in the Alps have built their lives and **livelihoods** from the tourism industry that these mountains attract. Although tourism is good for the **economy** it has created other problems such as pollution and **global warming**. The Alps are also rich in **natural resources**. The mountains were once renowned for their wealth of precious **minerals** that are mined from certain areas.

Snowboarding has become a popular winter sport in the Alps.

Les Menuires is located at an altitude of 6,100 feet (1,850 m) in the Three Valleys, in Savoy, France.

Tourism

The Alps are called Europe's playground because many people vacation there. In the past 100 years the number of visiting tourists has steadily grown, especially during the winter months. Today, it is estimated that the Alps draw around 100 million tourists a year. It is the second largest tourist destination in the world.

Tourists visit the Alps in the winter for sports such as alpine skiing, tobogganing, and snowboarding. In the summer, people enjoy activities such as hiking and mountain climbing. To accommodate so many tourists, the Alps have drastically changed in appearance. Many of the natural, lush forests and valleys have been built up, or urbanized, into busy, crowded living spaces with resorts, hotels, vacation homes, restaurants, and stores. Many residents living in the Alps depend on tourism economically.

A favorite winter destination for tourists is the Les Menuires ski resort in France. In 2011, it offered visitors the largest ski area in the world. It also guarantees visitors that there will be snow. The resort has artificial snow-making machines that make sure there is always enough of the white stuff to ski on. The Les Menuires resort can sleep up to 25,500 guests. It also offers visitors 90 stores and 48 restaurants.

Summer in the Alps

The Alps have fewer tourists in the summer than the winter. This is because most people like to spend time on the beaches instead of in the mountains. To bring in more tourists one ski resort in France, called Tignes, brought in truckloads of sand and made their own beach. Tignes is located at an altitude of 6,900 feet (2,103 m) and has the highest beach in Europe. This resort has hosted famous sporting events such as the 1992 Olympic Winter Games, and the world-renowned annual bicycle racing competition, the Tour de France.

(above) Tignes offers a variety of summer activities including beach football (rugby), mountain bicycling, and golf. (below) Tignes was also the finish of the 8th stage of the 2007 Tour de France.

There is more to the Alps than just skiing. Hikers from around the world come to the mountain range for the scenic trails that meander throughout Europe.

41

Mining

Mountains are great sources of rocks and minerals. People have been mining the Alps for over a thousand years in places such as Eisenerz, Austria. Eisenerz is a mining town located on the Erzberg mountain. Erzberg means "ore mountain" in German. The entire mountain is iron **ore** and instead of digging inside the mountain to mine the ore, it is mined from the outer edges and resembles a huge pyramid of steps.

FAST FACT

The cinnabar mine in Idrija (Idria), Slovenia, in the Julian Alps, was the second largest in the world. Cinnabar is the ore of mercury, the silver liquid substance used in standard glass thermometers. Cinnabar is no longer mined there today, but it is open for tours.

Tourists can sightsee around Erzberg mountain to view the mining tunnels and quarries. Tours are also available on the narrow-gauge railway, which was once used to transport the iron ore from Eisenerz to the city of Leoben.

Transport trailers carrying products and supplies are lined up waiting to enter Gotthard tunnel in Switzerland.

Climate Change

Global warming is occurring all around the world. It is an increase in the average temperature which leads to **climate change**. This includes the Alps mountain range, too. In some ways, global warming is increasing at an even faster rate in the Alps. This is because the millions of tourists that travel to resort areas in the Alps create a lot of traffic. Transport trailers bringing products needed by service industries for the tourists create even more traffic. Well-traveled roads to these mountain destinations are filled with a steady flow of vehicles that create toxic emissions.

About 50 million cars and 12 million trucks travel through the Alps each year. The height of the mountain range creates a barrier that contains the pollution and stops it from escaping. Even though tourism is important to the economy of the Alps region, it also creates more pollution and global warming.

Scientists estimate that global warming will cause Alpine glaciers to shorten and disappear. Alpine plants and animals that thrive in the cooler temperatures will have to move upward to greater altitudes and face possible extinction. Global warming will also shorten the seasons for tourist destinations, such as ski resorts.

Attention! Landslide! A sign in the Switzerland Alps warns visitors of possible landslides.

Hazardous effects

Global warming also creates hazardous mountain conditions such as landslides. Landslides occur when areas of permafrost thaw. Permafrost is an area of rock or soil that is permanently frozen. When these areas on a mountain slope warm up they release soil and rock that will fall and damage mountain towns, resort areas, roads, and railways.

Organizations such as the Alpine Initiatives work toward halting the building of more roads through the Alps, and limiting the amount of transport traffic. The International Commission for the Protection of the Alps (CIPRA) is another organization that works toward preserving the Alps.

NOTABLE QUOTE

"To be 70 years old is like climbing the Alps. You reach a snow-crowned summit, and see behind you the deep valley stretching miles and miles away, and before you other summits higher and whiter, which you may have the strength to climb, or may not. Then you sit down and meditate and wonder which it will be."

—from a letter written on March 13, 1877, by famous American poet, Henry Wadsworth Longfellow

TIMELINE

40,000,000 B.C.	Two tectonic plates, the Eurasian plate and the African plate, collide and begin pushing against each other with a force so great that they fold layers of Earth's crust upward and begin forming the Alps
110,000–8,000 B.C.	Earth is covered in ice during the last ice age. Near the end of it huge glaciers begin to shift and carve out large valleys and moraines.
48,000 B.C.	Neanderthals live in caves in the Alps
6000 B.C.	Humans begin creating petroglyphs, or art, in the Alps
500 B.C.	Travelers record going through the Great St. Bernard Pass in the Alps
218 B.C.	Hannibal leads his Carthaginian army across the Alps to attack Rome
800	Frankish King, Charlemagne leads his army to attack and defeat the Italians
1786	Michel-Gabriel Paccard and Jacques Balmat climb to the summit of Mont Blanc. They are the first men on record as ever having climbed the tallest mountain of the Alps.
1803	French consul, Napoleon Bonaparte, leads his army through the Great St. Bernard Pass to fight the Austrian army in Italy
1818	Mary Shelley's classic novel, *Frankenstein*, is published
1865	Five English mountaineers climb to the top of the Matterhorn. They are the first men recorded as climbing this dangerous mountain.
1880	Swiss alpine classic novel, *Heidi*, is published
1920	English poet, T. S. Eliot publishes his poem "Cooking Egg," which makes mention of the Alps
1924	The very first winter Olympic games are held in Tignes, France, in the Alps
1965	The Oscar winning movie, *The Sound of Music*, is released in theaters. The story is set in the Alps.
1991	Hikers discover the well-preserved body of Otzi the Ice Man— a man who had lived almost 5,000 years ago
2010	The Loetschberg Base tunnel is completed and becomes the world's longest train tunnel

GLOSSARY

adaptation A physical change that makes survival easier in a particular environment

alpine Something that is related to high mountain areas

altitude A measurement of height above sea level

archaeologist A scientist who studies ancient animals from their skeletal remains or fossils

climate The long-term weather conditions in an area

climate change A long-term, lasting change in the weather conditions in an area

conifer A tree that bears its seeds in cones and has needles for leaves

crust The outer part of Earth

deciduous A tree that sheds it leaves when the colder seasons begin

drainage basin The area where surface water from rain, snow, or ice collects to form a lake or river

economy The use of money and goods and their arrangement

fossils The remains of a plant or animal of a past time that is preserved in earth or rock

geologist A scientist who studies rocks to understand the history of Earth

global warming The gradual increase in Earth's temperature

graze To feed on growing grass

hibernate To rest for long periods of time during the winter months

Latin An ancient Roman language

livelihood A means of being able to support and provide the necessities of life for one's self and/or family

migrate To move to a new location or position

minerals Naturally occurring substances that come from the ground

moraine Stones and earth that are carried and deposited by a glacier

natural resources Materials found in nature that are valuable or useful to humans

ore A mineral which contains a valuable metal that can be extracted or mined

oxygen A colorless, tasteless, odorless gas, which forms about 21 percent of the atmosphere and is necessary for life on Earth

prevailing winds Winds that typically blow from one direction most of the time

remote Secluded, natural, and far away from human habitation

species A category or class in which plants and animals that share common characteristics are classified

tectonic plates Giant pieces of Earth's crust

temperate Describing a climate that is usually mild without extremely cold or extremely hot temperatures

transhumance A seasonal migration from one area to another by farmers and their animals

urbanization The state of becoming or being a highly populated area

watershed An area of land that drains its excess water into a river or river system

INDEX

FIND OUT MORE

BOOKS

Maynard, Charles W. *The Alps*. PowerKids Press, 2004.

Somervill, Barbara A. *The Awesome Alps*. Child's World, 2004.

Miller, Gary. *The Rhine: Europe's River Highway*. Crabtree Publishing Company, 2010.

WEBSITES

Kids.Net.Au: Encyclopedia: Alps
http://encyclopedia.kids.net.au/page/al/Alps

How Stuff Works: The Alps
http://geography.howstuffworks.com/
    europe/the-alps.htm

World Wildlife Fund: The Alps
http://wwf.panda.org/what_we_do/
    where_we_work/alps/

The Free Dictionary: Alps Mountains
http://encyclopedia.farlex.com/Alps+mountains